GRIEG

Four Pieces

for oboe and piano

edited and arranged

by

NICHOLAS BLAKE

CHESTER MUSIC

FOUR PIECES

I

Edited and arranged by
NICHOLAS BLAKE

EDWARD GRIEG

II

Edited and arranged by
NICHOLAS BLAKE

III

Edited and arranged by
NICHOLAS BLAKE

GRIEG

Four Pieces

for oboe and piano

edited and arranged

by

NICHOLAS BLAKE

CHESTER MUSIC

OBOE

FOUR PIECES

I

Edited and arranged by
NICHOLAS BLAKE

EDWARD GRIEG

Allegretto, dolce espressivo ♩=96

c. 2¼'

OBOE

II

Edited and arranged by
NICHOLAS BLAKE

Andante (♩ = 80)

Piano

mp molto legato ed espressivo

Ⓐ

p

mp   *mf*

Ⓑ

p cresc. e ben tenuto poco a poco

ten.

ff cant.   *fp*

ritard.

5

p espr.

c. 2¼'

III

Edited and arranged by
NICHOLAS BLAKE

† pause second time only

IV

Edited and arranged by
JANET CRAXTON

OBOE

c. 2½'

Più mosso ♩ = 100

FINE
c. 2½'

† pause second time only.

IV

Edited and arranged by
JANET CRAXTON

c. 2½'